T0114751

MIDLIFE MAZE

She Turned & Walked Across
the Floor with a Classic Elegance
& Old Fashioned Charm!
I Looked with Recognition of a
Beauty Aged By Life but
Unfettered by Times Passed!
A Real Lady of Style & Grace,
Proud, Dignified & Still
My First & Last Love!

by Norman Smith

authorHOUSE

AuthorHouse™
1663 Liberty Drive
Bloomington, IN 47403
www.authorhouse.com
Phone: 833-262-8899

Published by AuthorHouse 04/20/2023

ISBN: 979-8-8230-0452-7 (sc)
ISBN: 979-8-8230-0481-7 (hc)
ISBN: 979-8-8230-0451-0 (e)

Library of Congress Control Number: 2023905882

Print information available on the last page.

FOX

She's Sneaking In Like
She Snuck Out, a Vixen
Raiding the Rooster Shack!
Coming Home Innocent &
Pure as an Angel with a
Crooked Halo & Smelling
Like a Plucked Hen!

JACK HAMMER HEART

Leaps, Flips, Somersaults, Skips, Hops,
Jumps, Cartwheels, Rolling, Rocking,
Twisting & Turning Inside Out!
My Heart Pounding Like a Jack Hammer
& Beating like a Bass Drum ...
All I did was Touch Your Hand!

MORE OR LESS

She Said Stop but I Heard Go!
Her Eyes Said Slower
but My Heart Beat Faster,
Her Guard was Up, She Evaded My Lips
but I Advanced Without Worry as
Her Desire For Less
Made Me Want Her More!

LET ME IN

When Love Comes Knockin'
Will You Open the Door,
Let Me In, Let Me Pass
through, Give Me a Sign!
I'm Knockin' & Prayin'
so Will You Open the Door!

Your Sigh, Your Touch, Your Eyes,
Your Smile as Your Body Moved,
Your Warmth, Your Desire, My Life!

OUT OF CONTROL

I See You Again & My Mind Goes Blank,
My Ability to Function gone South & My
Eyes were Cloudy with Dim Visions &
My Lips Uttering Words without Thought!
Blood Rushing through Throbbing Veins as
My Temperature Rises with Excitement,
Weak Knees & Unsteady Legs Wobbling.
I See You Again & My Mind is Blank,
I'm Out of Control, Running on Fumes,
Crashing & Burning … I'm Helpless as
I See You Again & My Mind is Blank!

3

ODDS ARE

He Asked, "What are the Odds She'll Come Back?"
I Replied, "That's a Losing Hand, I'd Pass!"

FLEETING DAZE

The Crazy Pace of an Active Life can be
Overwhelming & Without Reward Unless
You Stop to Regroup & Reflect to Enjoy
Accomplishments & Good Deeds!
Time Passes as Life Escapes in Fleeting
Days, Aging Our Souls & Adding another
Memory to the Book We Write in Retrospect!

TO WHAT END

Pushing Against Time, Racing to What End,
Stopping to Ponder What If!
Hurry to Stay Ahead of Games Played in
Everyday Haste … Clocks Chime, Alarming
Bodies to Action Daily until Years Pass.
Blurred in Confusion to What End … Age Stops
Time & I have Raced to What End!

THEY SAY

Wanting Something & Needing Something
are Two Separate Things!
Whoever Uttered those Words of Wisdom
Never Meet You!
Needing & Wanting You Go Hand in Hand
as One Without the Other is a Quest
Unworthy of Pursuit!

I Fiddled Around & Played A Different Tune ... My
Strings are Frayed & My Bow Bent & in Need
of Your Loving Touch

TANGLED UP

Just as My Life became Simple & Easy
You Came Along & Complicated Everything.
I'm Living a Dream & Holding on Tight as
You Make My Life a Tangled Web of Love!

MEANT TO BE

What You are to Me is
Everything & Nothing We
have is Better if We are Apart.
You have Made this Man
Complete & Whole Again,
Displaying Our Love to the
World as it is Meant to be!

IS IT OVER NOW

There's Something You have on Your Mind & in
Your Heart … Maybe, We need to have a Heart
Talk about Your Mind … Are You Thinking of
Leaving, making a New Start … Do You want to
replace Me with Another! Is it Over Now
… Are You Closing Your Life to Me …
Is there Something You have on Your Mind?

HOPES & DREAMS

You Gave Yourself to the Milkman & You
Gave the Postman Your Hopes & Dreams!
You Sent the Plumber away in a Sea of Desire
but I know You'll be True to Me!

ISLAND GIRL

Her Dress was Flowing in the Summer Breeze,
Her Auburn Hair Glowing in the Morning Sunrise!
She Faded into the Dawn leaving Me Breathless by
Her Beauty … I Traced My Steps each Morning,
Searching in Vain for another Glimpse of the
Strange & Mysterious Figure once again! My Day
& Night Dreams sought Her Out as Desire & need
to know Her became an Obsession, Haunting My
Every Waking Moment!
A Mere of Glance of a Speeding Car & I was
Rewarded with a Vision of Cascading Auburn Hair
as it Passed & Stopped nearby … An Open Door
& She emerged Barefoot & Smiling …
"I've watched You at a Distance & I'm Alone on this
Island … Walk with Me & tell Me Your Story!"
I took Her Hand & My Dream & Obsession
became a Reality! … The Agonizing Ring of My
Alarm pierced My Sleep & Shook Me Awake
& I Rose Once Again to Seek Her Out!

8

STROLLING

Those Beautiful Eyes Stare at Me as You
let Me Know how much You Desire to be
Caressed & Loved … You lay Your Head
on My Lap & Give Me a Sigh & willing
nod as You Walk to the Door … I see the
excitement as Your Body trembles as I
rise to Join You for Our Daily Walk …
Unleashed & Untethered, just Us Two,
Strolling along the Boulevard Together!

SO WHAT

So What's the Game You're Playing –
So What's Your Next Move with My Heart –
So What's the Reward for Winning … being First –
So What do You Gain by Losing Everything –
You Could have Stopped at the Start!

LOVE LIFE

The Hard thing about Aging Out is Losing
Your Personal Identity, giving up hope of
Accomplishment & Aspiring to a Better Life!
Don't accept the inevitable fact of Death
having a grip on Your Conscience & Soul!
Your Hopes & Dreams Fade away as
Days & Nights slip by & Time becomes
Meaningless ... The Visible Evidence of
Your Passing should remain Evident with
You in the Picture! Your Life should be
Lived & not closed up in a Shoebox of
Photos to be cast aside, erasing Your very
existence! Learn to Love Life as God
intended to the very end!

FULL MOON

You took Me on a Joy Ride to Lovers Lane
& We Traveled the World Under a Full Moon.
You showed Me Everything a Man Dreams of!
We became One, Moving in Harmony Together!

GOING HOME

Floating Upwards, Cloud Bound
on Wings spread in Heavenly Joy,
singing Odes to Merciful Hands
unfurled in Welcome gesture,
waiting to Collect My Soul &
Peacefully guiding this Lamb Home.

FATED TO BE

Neither of Us noticed the Change.
What was Our Life, as Our Destiny
seemed fated to be one with each
other … Our paths merged with Times
passing. What is Real? What is not,
Where are You? I believed in You,
I believed in Our Love.
Why You changed Your Path will
forever haunt My thoughts as
Your Memory Fades.

Knowing You Love Me
Is All I Need To Know!

JELLO BRAIN

Did You ever stop to think but Your Brain went all Jello with the Prospect of Wasting Good Brain Cells as You Might need Them later for a Battle with Wits!

COOL RAIN

We were standing in a Crowd waiting
on a Bus to Nowhere when a Dark Cloud
opened up & poured a Cool Rain on
everyone … People scattered for Shelter
as Your Eyes caught Mine & We Laughed
as Our Faces reflected drops streaming like
Tears … She offered Me Her hand, enjoying
a chance meeting of Two lonely Souls
finding Joy in a Simple Life Moment.

BOUND TO YOU

Suffocating, Shackled & Chained to You,
Smothered, Drained & Feeling Blue …
No Way Out, No Escaping Your Hold …
Your Grip is Binding & Holding on
to My Soul & I should walk away …
But, My Love for You Makes Me Stay!

14

CHAMELEON
Sometimes I Rotate in the Right Direction & End Up at Your Door! Do You Do anything other than Change Your Mind?

NEVER MORE
What I wanted to say, I Failed to Convey, the Words Uttered came out Stuttered. Blank Looks & Stares let Me know for sure ... You misunderstood My intent as You Shut the Door! I knocked & rapped many Times over, gathered some Clover ... A Bouquet in Hand & I knocked again but the Silent Reply & I heard You Never More! A Quiet Shore with No Hand to Hold, I strolled along in Silence & felt the Vibration of a Call ... An old Friend & I'll think of You Never More!

Your Complete Infatuation & Adoration
You have for Me is well noted ... I don't
think You're taking My Desire for You
to Go Away very Seriously ... Will You
Please, Let Go Of My Leg!!

IN NEED OF REPAIR

The long abandoned House needed repair
& the overgrown Yard had long surrendered
to weeds & brush. The broken, wooden
Fence needed a mere push to make it
collapse as memories flooded back to a
time when laughter & joy radiated from
within those walls. My Family lived Life
there & now alone & looking like a lost
soul, I returned to My Past to make a
New start from My beginning!

GRAY

Rain pouring down from Dark Clouds,
Wind howling through the Trees as
puddles form … Streams fill & Leaves
Fly in disarray to destinations unknown.
A Lightless Night with no Moonglow
to Guide the Lost Souls Home again.

WINGS

An Angel with Wings ready to Fly
to heights above the Clouds,
Her Halo Glowing, Lighting Her way
across the Universe, over Oceans
deep & Mountains high …
soaring past Fields, Rivers & Earth's
Pastures of Green Forests full of Life …
An Angel with Wings ready to Fly
… So, Let Her Fly!

WE DANCE

Moving in Step, We become One with
the Music of Love. Our Hearts Beating
with no one else in sight … Our Eyes
open only to one another … We Dance!
Romantic Moods give way to Melodies
of Love as the room sways & Music Plays.
Your touch guides My every move,
rolling in unison, perfectly timed to
come Face to Face in Love … We Dance!
Our hands caressing, Our bodies one,
the Beat felt with no thoughts of tomorrow.
No Worldly worries, Just We two …
Embraced in Dance in hopes of a
Chorus unending … Together We Dance!
Quietness fills the air, the room stills,
Dancers leave the floor … We Linger,
the Music pulsating in Our Hearts as
We hold Our pose, slowly moving, unaware,
alone under the reflecting lights
… We Dance!

IS THAT YOU

Is that You, the Girl I knew,
when days past in Our Youth …
Your Face etched with Life's Travels &
Your Frame aged by Year's gone by …
Is that You, still moving with Grace,
smiling with Lips remembered.
Do You know Me, hands held,
laughing by the river, skipping
stones, running in fields of Flowers
in what seems to be so long ago …
Is that You … Did You say Hello?

WASTE OF TIME

What's the Point of a Pointless Affair?
No Love, No Hope, No Desire for
Future Times … Wasted Emotion,
Endless Heartache, Tears Shed …
What's the Point of an Affair without
Two-of-a-Kind … Two of One Mind,
Two Souls as One!

DON'T YOU SEE
Let Me Go Now,
Don't Hold On …
Let Go of My Heart!
Your Loving Me,
It was never meant to be!
Let Me go My way,
Didn't You know, Don't You see,
We were never meant to be …
We were over at the start!

UPSIDE DOWN
These are Times when Nothing makes sense,
Times when Everything seems Upside Down!
All the Plans unravel & weigh on You.
Nothing makes sense & every things a Blur
… I look in Your Eyes, You Smile,
Everything is right side Up again!

NIGHT MOON
Parked in the Moonlight, Top Down,
Two Heads become one …
Gentle Breezes rustle the Trees &
Stars Twinkle in a Crystal Sky &
Your Kisses Heating up My Heart!

DO THE DANCE

I Like Rockin' & Rollin'
I Like to Do the Dance,
Do the Dance, Do the Dance,
Do the Dance with You!
I can Reel, I can Boogie,
I can Swing & Shag Dance …
I like to Feel Your Body move
with the Rhythm of the Music,
Dance the Night away &
Feel Your Body sway!
Do the Dance, Get Romance
& Step Out with You!

LAUGHING HEART

Sitting here admiring the way Your
Laugh fills the Spring Air with Joyful
sounds … Happiness surrounds You
wherever You are! Cool Breezes Chill
the Outside & Trees sing songs that
echo all around … Playing endlessly,
Creating a Chorus of Natural Beauty
that only You can enhance with
Your Laughing Heart!

ROAMING SEEDY TOWN

Stray Dogs & Alley Cats, Homeless & Roaming Round ... Not Tagged or Collared & No Master to Please ... Just Hanging out on Streets in Seedy Town ... Howling at Strangers, Scratching for Fleas!
Stray Dogs & Alley Cats Hungry & Cold, Running on Empty ... Looking for Bones & Scraps ... Their only cares, what tomorrow will bring!
Sunshine, Markets full, No Rain to ruin the Mood ... Not Tagged or Collared ... Free to Roam Seedy Town!

NO WORDS

Sometimes You just know without a word, feeling distance & silence without a word … Sighs of a longing from within & a Heart longing for more than what has been … I want Your happiness & I'm gone without a word!

REV IT UP

Oh Yeah Baby!
You pushed My Buttons, Pulled My String, Jump started My Heart! Thought My Motor has Stalled & My Body had no Spark but You cranked the Chain & made Me Purr like a well tuned Engine …
Oh Yeah Baby!
You keep My Pistons in Time & My Pipes clean so I can run like a well-oiled Machine … Letting You drive Me to Heaven, shifting My Love into High gear & sending My Heart soaring …
On Yeah Baby!

CAN YOU HUSH

I don't need to hear You,
I Can't take it anymore …
Please stop talking!
My ears are pounding …
Please can You Hush!
Your words are echoing around
My Brain like a Hammer Nailing
Spikes in My Skull … You said
that You're gone so leave …
Don't Slam the Door
on Your way out …
Why are You still talking?

WHY NOT JUST BE

Some days are a blur of things done in
a daze of Living an Incomplete Life
without purpose … a multitude of Blindly
doing the expected … Why not take
the Path covered in Mystery & Intrigue
… Why not obey Your inner desires to
be more … Why worry about expectations
of designed Achievements … Just Be!

ETERNAL BLISS

You Hug the Juice
right out of My Soul,
Arms embracing My Body,
Holding My Heart!
Your Lips on Mine,
Breathlessly exhaling Desire,
Hearts Beating, Skin Warm
with Expectation as Moonlight
reflects in the Glow of Your Eyes!
Pleasure given freely, without
reservation taking Me to Heaven
in Eternal Bliss ... We Kiss!

THINKING ABOUT YOU

I Don't Always Think About You
except Every Hour, Every Day ...
You're Never on My Mind,
Just 24 Hours, Seven Days a Week!
The Images Etched into My Brain
of You & Me are fading away.
But Your Picture is in Clear Focus
in My Mind's Eye!
I Don't Always Think About You
except Every Hour, Every Day!

COMING UP ACES

We Rolled the Dice,
Flipped the Coins &
Cut the Cards … Luck &
Good Times & We came
Up Aces! We Gambled,
Took a Chance on Love,
Bet the House on Our Hearts
& Won Life's Lottery!

A PASSING STORM

We Live like tomorrow is a Sunrise Away
as Time Vanishes like a Passing Storm.
Today is Gone in an Instant & We can
only Dream about what might have been.

YOUR PROFILE

Blood rushed to My Head & My Heart
Beat in anticipation of seeing You again,
Our Digital Connection would become a
Reality as Your Profile Comes to Life!

There was a Moment when Everything
Made Sense & Nothing was Out of Place!

29

CABANA ON THE STRAND

Your Behind Swaying in
Directions kind to the Eyes
& just above Smooth &
Tanned Thighs, Walking
through the Sand, Leaving Prints,
"Follow Me to My Cabana"
Lotion Reflecting Sunlight off
Sculpted Skin God Created …
an Image Men Desire to Devour
but Untouchable, Unattainable
to All! You Torture My Vision
& Steal My Soul, hoping the
Footprints were meant for Me &
said, "Follow Me to My Cabana"

OUT TO PASTURE

Cows Low, Sheep Baa, Horses
Neigh, Pigs Oink … I'm Out to
Pasture, Farmed Out, Baled &
My Desire is Plowed Under
& My Seed all Sowed! Barns,
Silos & Fences everywhere I Look!
Cows Low, Sheep Baa, Horses
Neigh & Pigs Oink … Hens Cackling,
Corn Shucking … I'm Rocking,
I'm Out to Pasture, Smiling &
Smelling Chicken on You!

Did You Lose My Number
You Never Called, You Promised to Call ...
You have My Number ... I'm Waiting!

A REAL LADY

She Turned & Walked across the Floor with
a Classic Elegance & Old Fashioned Charm!
I looked with recognition of a Beauty Aged
by Life but Unfettered by Times Passed!
A Real Lady of Style & Grace, Proud &
Dignified & Still My First & Last Love!

GLOWING EMBERS

Embers Glow in the Twilight surrounded by
Tinder just waiting to be ignited into a Flame
of Life to Light Up the Night again!
Her Eyes are Embers that Desire Loves Match!

AN ANGEL SPEAKS

Just heard a Voice from My Past! My Heart Stopped!
Just a few words, "Hello, How are You doing?"
Just Melodic tones from a Voice remembered!
Just a Sweet Song Sung from an Angel long silent,
Just a Stranger talking to another! My Heart Stopped!

A MYSTERY TO ME

It was becoming quite clear that My current situation was as dire as it could be! I had taken a turn onto Gravel Road seldom used … My tracks making an impression easy to follow. The Ominous looking Black SUV with the obscure Windows had followed Me from Home. Whoever was inside was a Mystery & I was Clueless what had attracted Them to Me. With Careful deliberation, My intent was to remain under cover … something or someone had discovered Me & now They were closing in! Thinking back to Yesterday, I could only surmise that She had enticed Me into Her Web of Desire with ill intent. Somehow She had gotten in touch with Her Comrades. I pulled over into a Grove of Aspens with expectations that this could be the end! The Black SUV stopped & She exited the backseat fully armed with a Bouquet of Yellow Roses, a beautiful Lace Wedding Dress, Her Dad close behind! The Aspen Grove filled with Music & Laughter as I straightened My Tie … I came to the Conclusion that Tomorrow, I would become a Man possessed & Single No More!

LEAP OF FAITH

Knowing You has given
New life to a Dead Soul -
Believing in You & Giving
all without fear of rejection -
Taking a Leap of Faith
into Loves Unknown Path -
Brings an Old Heart Full Circle
with Childlike Wonder!

PASSIONATELY YOURS

What would You say if I said,
"I Love You!"
Am I wrong to feel Passionate about You
… I feel Chained to Your Heart &
Connected to You Physically …
What would You say if I said,
"I Love You!"

Rocky Times are Behind Us
Good Sailing on Ocean Tides,
Sunlight Warming Our Souls,
Sailing Back into Love Again!

BETTING ON LIFE

I looked for a place to relieve Myself of Morning Coffee & a movement startled Me! A quiet Voice whispered, "Where You heading Mister?" ... I gathered Myself & replied, "Vegas!" An Ancient, withered figure emerged, etched in time but with a knowing smile, "Been to Vegas, won a fortune & odds are, will go again ... what's Your story?" My story unraveled as I felt the need to tell this stranger about My life ... I was a Hometown Hero, athlete, Soldier of Fortune Who fought a War & returned to Wed the Girl I left behind ... A Homecoming Queen for Life with an innocent Glow of the Girl next door ... She had promised to be True & My excitement overflowed as I exited the Train only to find an empty Depot ... The Taxi took Me to Her Door as I anticipated a Soldier's Welcome ... I knocked to find My Best Friend whose Guilty look was all I needed to Know! Now, I'm heading to Vegas, betting on starting over, winning a New Life without My Homecoming Queen!

She's a Pigeon ... Cooing all over the Place & Crapping on Everything & Everybody!

LET'S DANCE

It was with curiosity that I watched
as You Danced across the Floor with
effortless Motion ... Your Peaceful &
Comfortable Grace told a Story of
Happiness & a Secure Nature ...
You stopped Pensively in thought as
if a momentary idea had crossed Your
Mind ... Once more, You smiled &
continued Your Dance, a stranger to no
one ... gesturing hands, welcoming
conversation, no one unfriendly ... You
stopped & turned, Eyes searching
the room, expecting a familiar face in
the crowd ... Coming closer ... You
stopped, extended Your hand & said,
"Let's Dance" & We Danced!

Ok ... I Agreed to a Little Strip-Poker &
All Night Darts but I Do have My Dignity!

SIMPLY SAID

It was Closing Time at Dave's & My need
for alcohol had, long ago, exceeded it's limits!
The Barkeep took My Glass & signaled for Me
to pay up so He could go home ... Moonlight
painted an eerie scene of Dancing Shadows as
a light rain fell, damp & cold ... Dave's had
become a Nightly Ritual since She walked out,
taking My Hopes & Dreams with Her ...
Nothing about it made sense as She never
showed Me anything but Happiness, Warmth
& Desire ... Trouble was, She just left, leaving
a note, "Sorry, Goodbye" ... Days became a
Blur & Nights, Sleepless, Restless & a testament
to My Loneliness ... I Stumbled up the Steps,
fumbling for My Keys, slowly becoming aware
that I wasn't alone! Her Form came into Focus
& She reached for My Hand & simply said,
"Don't ask" & I never did! We shared Happiness,
Warmth & a Lifetime of Desire as Dave's became
a distant memory!

EMOTIONS

If Red was the color of Your Eyes & if
Your Mood was Cold & Blue like Burnt Embers
… If Your Heart was beating out loud & clear
telling all about Your Emotional Roller Coaster
… would Ocean Waves calm Your Mind & could
an Ocean Breeze ease Your painful Memory
… Can ebbing Tides of Peace & Calm bring
new Hope, Love & Joy Your way again …
Can I be the Man that relights Your Glow … Can
I walk with You in Sunshine & Moonlight … Let
Me Love You Until the Breaking of a New Dawn.

41

OIL & WATER

You're a Honey, Hugs & Hold Me kind
of Woman ... I'm a Beer, Bourbon & Ball
kind of Man ... We're Oil & Water ...
Fire & Ice... Leather & Lace ... I'm
a Sensitive Man Who can Do the Dance
... So Let's Wine, Dine, Walk & Talk ...
Let's Mix It Up & Kiss!
I'll Hug & Hold You ... Drink Your
Wine & Dine You... I'm a Sensitive
Man Who can do the Dance ... do the
Dance ... So take a chance on Romance
... Let's Mix It Up & Kiss!
I like My Beer, Bourbon & Ball ... I'm
that kind of Man ... You like Your Honey,
Hugs & Hold Me Tights ... I like to Hang
Out with the Boys, Play All Night ... But,
I'm a Sensitive Man Who can Do the Dance
... So Let's Wine, Dine, Walk & Talk, So
... Let's Mix It Up & Kiss!
I'll Hug & Hold You ... Drink Your Wine
& Dine You ... I'm a Sensitive Man Who
can do the Dance ... do the Dance
So take a chance on Romance
... Let's Mix It Up & Kiss!

I Politely Inquired,
"Is Your Body Untouchable anywhere?"
She politely took My hand & said,
"There, There, There & Oh Yes ... Right There!"

His Youthful Exuberance Evaporated as
Her Grip On His Manhood Tightened!

SIREN

The Lowest Place, the Endless Regret,
Sorrow & Tears will never compare to
Your Heartless Mind that tore My Soul
& left Me half the Man I used to be.
Your outward Beauty, Your willing smile
were just an act rehearsed & displayed
… the Mask removed, reveals a calloused
Siren with hatred disguised as allure!
You reached inside My Chest & from
it, My Heart You tore!
My Blindness for Your Love destroyed
the Man I was & You Waltzed over Me
in My Cloudy Haze … What saved a
Drowning Clown, walking with Empty Eyes
peering back at Me with a Demons Daze!
I startled awake from Dreams of Your
Physical Beauty as absence dulls My
dire sensibility … I smile as Reality
forms & Your Image Fades Away.

OUR FAVORITE SONG

Strollin' on the Strand with My Lifetime Best Friend,
Holding Hands like Kids, Leaving Footprints in the
Sand ... No worries about Life ... Just sharing Smiles
on the Beach where We belong, Livin' out Our favorite
Song! Whispers of Sound all around, Dancers Steppin'
in time, Rollin' in each others arms, strollin' in Love
to Our Hearts Beating as One ... Heaven on Earth in
Paradise together on the Beach where We belong
... Livin' out Our favorite Song!
You make Me Young again in a place where no one
worries about tomorrow ... Dancin' on the sand,
once more, Barefoot on the Strand ... Holding
each other like kids ... Livin' out Our favorite song!

DAWN'S LIGHT

Dancing Rays reflect on Vibrant Leaves,
Dew Drops glisten on Morning Foliage.
Quietness disturbed by only the Wind,
whispering to waken Nature's Creatures
from Silent Slumber ... Darkness gives
way to Colorful Clouds of Radiant Light
shimmering over a Distant Horizon
... Another Day to Live.

REPOSE

She Yawns, stretching, rising to meet
the day ... Her Silhouette posing Angelic
before a shadeless Window.
Her Hair flowing wistfully in Sleepy
Tresses ... Gown's Satin threads sculpting
Beauty only God could form. A Dream
My Eyes desire to Caress forever!

Our Love Has No Boundaries ... Except That!

PASSIONATE HEARTS

It wasn't always like this … There was a
time when Moonlight Walks & Candlelight
Dinners helped give credibility to Their
Affair … Promises of tomorrow & late night
Passionate meetings & Glowing Embers
warming Loving Hearts.
He would tell Her soon & that His Loveless
Life would end & They could build a
New Life together!
There was a knock on the door & She
was Beautiful & Her Smile disarming as
She said, "I'm leaving Him & making a
New Life for Me … He came into Our
Marriage with Nothing & I'm leaving Him
the same way … I'm telling You this because
I left a good Man to be with Him!
She turned, smiled & walked away!
Yes, It wasn't always like this & My Man
said, "Who was that?" … I smiled &
replied, "No One, Can I fix You a Drink!"

49

DESIRE

Everyone likes the Smiling Face, Easy Laugh
& putting on a Party Demeanor ... Soothing
Music & Dancers acting out ritualistic mating
expressions & desires!
Popping the Top on another Lager, I made
My way through the Curtained Doorway into
the Cool Night Air.
She was standing by the water, bare Skin
reflecting the Glimmering Light off Her Silky
Auburn Hair ... Her glance caught Me staring
& She motioned Me forward ... I smiled &
laughed as I willingly fell into Her Web to
become a Victim of this Enchanting Creature!

LOW-DOWN BLUE

You Left Me High & Dry …
Now I'm Drowning in My
Low-Down Blue Tears
over You! You Left to find
Yourself & I'm Still
Drowning in Heartbreak City,
Blue & Low-Down over You!

ALL FUZZY, ALL OVER

Dizzy, Dazzled & Frazzled &
Sizzling, Burning & all Fuzzy Inside
… You are My Soulmate, Feeling all
Jazzy, Warm all over & Plucking My
Heart Strings & Pinging My Brain.

PEACEFUL SLUMBER

Laying with My Eyes shut tight,
Dreaming, wanting to keep My
Peaceful Slumber while Images
of You Dance Through My Mind!

DO THAT THING

That Thing You DO
When You Do That Thing,
Turns Me Around &
Upside Down & Outside In!
You Confuse My Love
with Serious Like,
All I Need is More of
That Thing You Do!

REGRET

My Life is a Six Pack of Regret
Since I Let You Fly Away Into His Arms

JUST A SMILE

The Neon Lights of an All Night Dinner
Flashed in the haze of drizzle on My Windshield
… the Wipers had Me ready for Hot Coffee & rest
as My Eyelids drooped with a days staring at an
endless Highway … Parking & exiting in a Gush
of Wind & Rain, I opened the Diner Door.
The place was nearly empty with a mellow
Country Ballad on the Jukebox & the rattle of
dishes coming from the Kitchen … An Elderly
Couple sat in the corner booth as I took a seat
at the Counter, trying to focus on the soiled
Menu with typical Diner Food … A Kitchen
door swung open & She appeared with a
glance My way & a smile that made My
Heart Leap … Her Blue Eyes shown & I maybe
stared too long as She delivered the couples
order … I looked down at My Hands & looked
at My image in the Diner Mirror … A pretty
sad, tired & worn out Man on the Road to
Nowhere … My Life back in Toledo had hit
Rock Bottom & here I was expecting nothing
but feeling that old excitement of a Young
Heart surfacing … The Coffee was Hot &
Apple Pie tasty as We exchanged pleasantries
… I thanked Her & head South renewed &
bearing the image of a Diner Waitress, giving
Me a reason to Hope & Dream again!!

NEW DAY

I open My Eyes from Dreams unclear,
remembered briefly in distant shadows,
thoughts Clouded as Summer wakes.
A New Day greets & visions appear as
Sunlight filters through Curtains sheer,
dancing across the room in warm rays.
Content I turn, caressing Your body gently,
greeting a New Day Full of Life once more.

RUNNING FREE

Rising to heights unatainable, giving
Body & Soul to efforts not rewarded,
seeking a road discovered by chance.
Never taking lightly a Life Free to Run,
unteathered by bonds others accept as
Naturally given as how it is to be.

SUNRISE, SUNSET

Somewhere, while Walking
We wondered where Time
would lead Us, What Path We
would take. Would We walk as
one into each Sunrise or go
Our separate ways ... exploring
new Adventures & meet at Sunset
at some distant Oasis!

FEELING BLESSED

Sometimes I wander alone with My thoughts,
Breathing in Fresh Air & exhaling Life's Gift
into the Night, feeling Blessed to know You!

OCEAN TIDES

Change of Heart & altered Plans, Events
making paths unclear & out of focus,
Walking down a Sea Oats & Sandy Trail
of Soft Dunes ... Listening to the roar of
Ocean Tides & walking on a Sandy Beach,
a Warm Breeze blowing & thoughts of You
running through My Mind & I Smile!

You Blew Over Me Like a Tumbleweed & Left Me in Your Dust!

MOLASSES

I melted like Molasses the first time We kissed & My Soul sweetened like Honey on a Hot Biscuit the first time We embraced ... I was Yours after Midnight & in the Light of a New Dawn as You were an Angel touching My Body with Your Heart!

SITTEN'

My Ole Dawg "Bone" & I were hanging out & Howlin' at anything that moved! The Sun was Warm & the Creek Water rustling over Rocks making Our Day perfect for Sitten' ... A Cool Breeze blew through the Trees adding to a Day made for relaxing with nothing else to do as Ole' "Bone" dozed off & I Drifted off into Dreamland!

YOUR LAST LOVE

Your Last Love Broke Your Heart & left You Crying! You show Me where You fell in Love, how You Danced, Laughed & ran Wild & Free! Open Your Eyes, see Me ... I want to make My Own Dreams so tell Me about Your New Love & how We Dance, Laugh & run Wild & Free!

WHAT'S HER NAME

Sometimes, Her Name rolls off My Tongue
like a Bowling Ball dropping on My Bare Foot.
Her Name is etched into the Fibers of My being
… Deeply cutting Fissures across My Heart Walls
Yodeling & Echoing in My Throbbing Brain!

NEW HORIZONS

Today, I run towards, I know not what …
escaping four walls that trapped Me inside
… Looking to change the course I've taken!
Seeking New Horizons to enlighten My Soul,
Hoping to find Peace, Serenity & a New Start.

RELEASE ME

All knotted up & tied
to Your every move,
Your Love Strings tugging at My Heart
... Arrows of Emotional Bonds
have Me in Chains ... My Head
is spinning as Your Web tightens!
Release Me & Free My Soul ...
Don't take My Passion away!

PICKING DAISES

A little Homespun & Down Home Country,
Howdy-Do friendly with a Wholesome air.
Running through Golden & Dusty Cornfields,
Your Pearly Whites beaming from a glowing
Smile ... Picking Daisies & Dancing, Skipping
on Bare Feet, Your Sundress flowing to settle
with grace into Your Porch Swing ... Plucking
Petals One by One, "He Loves Me, He Loves
Me Not, He Loves Me ... Yes I Do!"

STUCK LIKE GLUE

Even though You're with Someone New,
It Seems like only Yesterday We were
"Stuck Like Glue"
Do You Remember the things We did
Together ... How did We let it slip away!
It Seems like only Yesterday We were
"Stuck Like Glue"

Lustfully, She Lavished His Limbo –
Gustily, He Ground Her Petals –
Sensually, Satisfied, They Shimmered –
Seductively within Eden's Gates ...
Rays of Golden Sunlight spread
across Gleaming Limbs!!

PARTY HATS

Let's put on Our Party Hats, find a Place
where Friends are Friendlier, Wine is Finer,
Beer is Colder where We never act older!
Bring Yourself or Someone Else & leave
Your Attitude at Home …
Let's find a Party Place together & Dance
Til' the Cows come Home!

HEARTBEATS

Gracefully Charming, Deliciously Sweet,
Sunlight Dancing off Your Silky Hair
… Reflections shining in Smiling Eyes
… Bodies gliding across Warm Sands,
Footprints washed away by Ocean Tides,
Your Breath on My Cheek …
My Heart Skips a Beat.

DEAR RONNIE

After Lunch today, I went to John's Office to order some supplies ... He wasn't there! So, I went to see Glen ... He wasn't there! I went to Ralph's Office to see when Glen would return ... He wasn't there! I went to Frank's Office & He'd left for Vegas ... Wayne was off playing Golf ... Bob & Harold were both Out of Their Offices ... Went to See Bill to talk to Him but ... He wasn't there! Then, I went by Your Office & You weren't there either ... Clay & Fred were gone ... I went to Mr. Sublette's office ... He & I decided there was a Bomb Scare ... We Left!! Regards, Don

PS: I Had this Memo typed outside as Nancy wasn't there either!

cc: Ronnie, John, Glen, Frank, Wayne, Bob, Harold, Bill, Clay, Fred, Francis & Nancy!!

FAST BALL

The wait seems forever as I take My turn
Scanning the Playing Field ... All Eyes,
Hearts & Hopes resting on Dreams of
Glory long desired but Never achieved!
Chattering Voices chant relentlessly as
Gloves Pound, focused on Final Victory
... The Ball appears from a Reliever's
Practiced Arm ... No Breaking Path or
Change Detected ... Just Heat Blazing a
Trail towards Home, The Bat's Cracking
Sound is a Deafening Reward!

THIS TIME

This Time, I ain't Foolin', I'm Standing My
Ground, So Don't say I didn't warn You Girl
... This Time!
Don't try that Silly Stuff on Me, I've made up My
Mind ... Come any Closer, the Deal is Done ...
You know I'm Not Lying ... turn those Lips around!
This Time I Ain't Fallin' in Love with You
... Again! This Time, I'm Not going to be Your Fool
... This Time!
Take those Lips & Your Perfumed Neck ... Those
Tender Arms full of Charms ... Graceful Legs &
Those Eyes ... I Ain't Foolin' & I ain't Fallin' for
Your Heart No more ... at least Not This Time ...
There You Go & There I Go ... One more time
around the Dance Floor ... Movin' to Our Song ...
This Time I Ain't Fallin' for You any more ...
Until Next Time!

She Motioned Me Towards Her
She Moved Her Lips & Blew Me a Kiss
... She turned & Walked Away &
Wiggled just right & Made My Day
... She must have thought I'd Lost My Mind
as I Just Stood there with My Mouth
wide open, Aware of what I'd Miss!!

LUCKY DOG

As I Scratched the "Lucky Dog" Lotto Ticket, My anticipation of Winning elapsed with each reveal of a losing number ... My need for a "Big Win" had become elevated as My Girl found refuge in the arms & life of another Man ... He was more than rich in both wealth & in His youthful exuberance ... My old Rambler & rundown, overgrown Home were befitting a beaten down, shadow of a worn out Man that I had become ... As I revealed a couple more losing numbers, the change in My pocket spared Me any ability to buy another chance! One more scratch & I would discard both the card & My Girl into file thirteen ... My Eyes cleared as a "20X" appeared & as I trembled with anticipation, "One Million" ... No ..."20 Million" & suddenly I knew exactly what to do ... Later, in 1st Class, I watched as a Beautiful Lady of some standing came towards My seat ... She whispered, "Is this Seat taken & are You Taken?" ... I replied, "No, I'm just a Lucky Man that's Free & No, I'm Not taken anymore!"

HERE I AM

You Forgot To Shut The Door ...
Here I Am Standing Outside!
You Kissed Me & Made Me Want More,
Here I Am, Standing Outside!
Should I Come In ... Is There More?
I Still Feel your Lips On Mine ...
Here I Am Standing Outside!
Should I Come In, What's On Your Mind
... The Night Is Young & Here I Stand,
Come In You Whispered, Be My Man!

Today I am a Man of Age ... Paid My Dues,
Worked all My Life & I've had the Blues
... When I put on My Dancing Shoes,
I'm a New Man with nothing to Lose ...
The Ladies Sway ... I become a Happy Man
When I put on My Dancing Shoes!

BESSIE BOVINE

She likes Farm life & lazy, crazy days
Grazing … Bessie "Mooed" when We
Hugged & I'm amazed at Her Demeanor
… It's Utterly fascinating how You
Moseyed through the Kitchen & Chewed
Your way into My Refrigerator …
Even My last piece of Apple Pie fell
victim to Your Gullet … That's the
last time I'll Date Anyone from
www.ucudbmine.com

Our Night was full of Dance & Wild Passion as
I Smelled the Aroma of Fresh Brewed Coffee ...
I was Dreaming of "Breakfast in Bed & Got Up,
Our Evening of Whiskey & Romance on My Mind!
You Appeared like an Angel with a "To Go" Cup!

KATIE

Oh Dog of Dots that Speckle Your Hide, Why
in My House Do You Abide ... with Teeth that
Chew My favorite Shoe & Gnaw upon My Leg
so Tender ... You Lay contented upon My Lazy
Boy ... What sort of Devious Deviltry awaits on
My Personal affects to Render ... No Dotted
Canine can spoof affection ... Smirkly Snip &
Slobber ... I think it reasonable to assume My
Heart You've Managed to
Disassemble with Big Eyes
that Melt My Resolve & a
Tearful Reunion ... Best
Friends We Resemble!!

KILLING TIME

Isn't it strange how some insignificant thing can change the direction of Your Life without explanation! My Breakfast was a simple Daily habit of Hot Coffee & a Breakfast Pastry while sitting at My usual outside table, killing Time before My morning Ritual began. As the day Dawned, a Shaggy Creature, dragging a Leash, jogged towards Me! It's tired Tongue needed quenching & it gladly lapped up the water from My cup. A friendly voice said, "So, there You are Max!" I looked up into the Bluest Eyes I had ever encountered! Today, We sit together with Max, enjoying Our Hot Coffee & Breakfast Pastries at Our usual outside table, killing time before, Our Morning Ritual!

Each Day, I Wonder, What Have I Left Undone
... Did I Create New Memories ...
Did I Make Someone Smile!

NO ONE SAID

No One Said it would Happen like this -
No One Said I would fall so hard -
No One Said Time would stand still -
No One Said My Heart had wings -
No One Said I should Walk away -
No One Said I would fall so hard!

Dating Her was like Driving on
a Long Trip with No Exit Plan …
Yield, Stop, Keep Right, Detour,
Proceed with Caution … Make a
U-Turn … Must have been a
Traffic Jam on this Road Before!

NO REGRETS

You turned Me Inside Out,
Upside Down, took Me to an
Oasis of Serene Emotion …
You flipped My Passion to
the "On" Position,
I lost Control of the Situation
… You gave Me renewed Faith
that Love could be had again
without regret! Pure Elation
… You turned this Man Inside
Out & Upside Down &
I lost Control of the Situation!

You Showed Up at My Door
Wearing a Smile & Nothing More!

MANLY THINGS

You asked Me a Question ... Your Words Escaped
My Brain ... Something about Love ... Your Lips
are Moving & You asked Me a Question!
I don't have Words about Love!
So, if You Love Me, ask Me about Manly things
like Fishing, Hunting, Trucks, Cars, Beer or Bars!
Ask Me about Manly things ... Just Don't ask Me
about Love, Romance or the Stars ...
Yes, I Love Your Dress, Your Hair & Your
Shoes & Can We Go Now ... well ... maybe not!

I thought Life had run it's course ... a Wild ride
on a Wild Horse, Time & Nature have Wrinkled
My Face & My Body Trampled all over the Place
... Friends & Lovers come & They go like Ocean
Tides on a Sandy Shore ... The Hourglass turned
over again & She touched My Heart &
I am a Man alive once more!

ACHIN' HEAD BLUES

If You'd Quit Talking for a maybe a Minute,
I could think without listening to You Dear!
Give Me a second to Remember what You Said
… it would help if "You'd Pass Me My Beer!"
My Heads Aching, My Ears Buzzing & My
Brain is in Pain … Your Words are running
around My Head … You're Gone
… "Where's My Beer!"
Some Days I have a Grip & then I Slip,
no warning signs to see … I'd Stop My
Drinking if You'd Quit Yakking … Let it Be!
You say You'll leave Me if I don't Change
… Time is slipping away … There's not
enough Beer in this World to make Me stay!
Did the Door just slam … My Brain's in a Daze!
My Heads Aching, My Ears Buzzing & My
Brain is in Pain … Your Words are running
around My Head … You're Gone
… "Where's My Beer!"

DUCKING VARMINTS

There We were, just Me & My Ole Mule against a Hoard of Claim Jumpers ... Only thing between Me & keeping My Gold was finding someplace to skedaddle to from here ... I had seen a Bear Cave back yonder & I took off Quick as Ole Mule could run! Must have been six or seven Varmints swarming like Mad Wasps on My Tail ... Me & Ole Mule ducked into that lair & came face to face with Mamma & Her Cubs ... I left as Quick as I had entered, full speed right past those Crooks ... Last Glance, They were high-tailing it South with Mamma right on Their Tail! Me & Ole Mule took Our Gold to Town in Need of some Strong Libation & Pleasant Company!

Redundancy & Repetition are the Bane of Our Existence!

MOVING OUT

I Got Tossed Out & Locked Out,
Moved Out & Now, I'm Going Out!
Everything I Knew about You was
left inside that closed Door & Now,
It's Healing Time ... Time to
move on to find Something More!
I'm Moving Out & Going Out ...
Hoping to Heal a Wounded Heart!
I'm Moving Out & Going Out ...
This Man is Making a New Start
You tossed Me Out & Locked Me Out,
I'm Moving Out & Going Out ...
It's time to Heal a Wounded Heart!

DREAM DANCING

Dream Dancing & Walking on Air,
Misty Visions of Souls United in time
… Floating on Clouds in Love as One,
Dream Dancing & Walking on Air!
Dreaming of Strolling on Sandy Shores,
Holding Hands & Gently Touching …
Shadows cast & Images shimmering,
Dream Dancing of Romance & You.
Dream Dancing & Wishing on a Star,
Imagining You & I Romance Dancing
… Together forever by the Ocean
Until the Warm Sun Rises Again!

DO YOU LOVE ME

You Ask, "Do You Love Me?"
You don't touch Me like You used to do!
Where is that caress, that whisper
… Where did that Breathless Sigh Go!
Where is Your Love …
How do I make You desire Me again
… You Ask, "Do You Love Me?"

LIFELINE
Livin' on the Low Road,
Dreamin' of the High Road,
Lookin' Like a Fool,
Lost in a Mindless Fog ...
You Threw Me a Lifeline
and Lifted a Heavy Load,
Lighting My Path back to
Believing in Love Again!

THE PARK BENCH

An Eagle was Drifting across a Clear Blue
Sky and a Warm Breeze rustled the Leaves
... The Park Bench was sheltered just off the
path in a Beautiful Aspen Grove ... It seemed
I closed My Eyes for just an instant as a Voice
whispered softly, "Would You Mind If I sit
awhile?" ... She was just a Young Girl in a
Floral dress with long tresses that flowed
in the wind. I motioned for Her to sit as
She spoke again, "We always Loved this
spot & He said, that, one day He would
return ... the War took Him from Me so I
come here daily so His Memory won't fade!"
... We sat in silence for a long time as the
Eagle soared & the leaves rustled above!

"Tell Me What's the Matter!"

NSmith

HAYLIE

HAYLIE-AUTISM

Haylie is the "Autistic Angel" & Aspergers child that is a Joyful, Artistic, Intelligent young Girl ... She has Typical Traits related to Autism & has Her "Meltdown Moments" of confusion & often asks, "Tell Me What's the matter!" ... I have included the "Haylie-Autism" pages to help give insight into, maybe, what She's Feeling ... She wears Her "Kids Ears" & loses Herself when connected to "Alexa" & Youtube & being a V-Tech Queen keeps Her in a Fantasy World of Escape from Reality ... The Artist has had Custody & spends time Drawing, Reading & trying to "Cope" with Haylie's Special Needs ... another part of His "Midlife Maze!"

Haylie

My Autistic Angel

HAYLIE-AUTISM
Let's Go On A Mission Just Us Two, to the Mall or Wherever We End Up, "Just The Two Of Us!"

ARE YOU OK

Sometimes My World of Thoughts & Visual
Stimulants Collide into a Sensory Overload
… My Focus wanders into Total Confusion …
I Scream & Hit Myself in Frustration & Ask,
"What's Wrong?"
Please Sit or Stand or Hold My Hand,
Don't ask again, "Are You OK?"

A NEW DAY TO BE ME

I Make My Lunch & Dress Myself, Slip
on My Shoes & I'm Ready to Go!
My Teeth & Hair are Brushed & I'm
Ready for School … My Smile all Glowing!
From the Backseat with My "Kids Ears" On
… I Watch the World Go By in a Blur of
Color … I Hope My Friends will Smile at
Me Too … There's My Teacher …
Into The School I Go!

HAYLIE-AUTISM

This Goes Here, This Goes There
Here & There, There & Here,
Line it Up One by One in a Row!
Where is the Green Block ...
Oh No, There it is, On the Floor
... Hey Green Block, You Go Here!

EVERYDAY GIRL

Just an Everyday Girl in Everyday Clothes,
Living My Everyday Life in Everyday Ways.
Doing Everyday Things with Everyday People,
Having an Everyday Good Time ... Everyday!

TUNED OUT

Plugged in & Tuned Out with Devices
all about ... I'm a V-Tech Queen that
Loves anything that "ABC's or 123's"
with Games that Sing & Melodies that
Repeat, Repeat, Repeat & Repeat!
Androids, Phones, Computers Connected,
Plugged in, Tuned Out ... Devices all about!

HAYLIE-AUTISM

Old McDonald Had A Farm!
I Should Know ... I Listen & Watch
Over, Over, Over & Over Again!
Well ... You Get the Picture!
Repeating Seems to be a Habit of Mine
... A Habit of Mine ... Baa Baa!

My Connections are Far & World Wide ...
I Can be Myself or Anyone Else & Explore
a Magic Forest or the Deep Blue Sea ...
I Can Go Sailing, Flying or Riding a Whale
or Swim with Dolphins or Ride the Rail!
I can go alone or take a Friend ... Who can
Hold My Hand ... "Will You Hold My Hand?"

Looking around My World of One, My
Door is Closed ... I Sit on My Bed
Surrounded by My Make Believe Friends.
Stuffed & Staring back at Me in Silence!
They need to be Held & Hugged & They
Like to Hug Me Back ... Some Need to
tell Me ... "Change My Batteries!"

HAYLIE-AUTISM

Wonder Where Everyone Went ...
Big Kids, Little Kids Everywhere!
Running, Walking, Laughing, Yelling
... Up the Stairs, Down the Hall &
Vanishing Through Open Doors!
Big Kids, Little Kids Without a Trace
... "Can I Come Too?"

YOU THINK

You Think You're Talking to an Empty Mind,
You Think I Can't Hear the Things You Say,
You Think Because I'm Not Looking Your Way,
You Think I Don't See Your Stares & Glares,
You Think I'm Special ... I Know, I'm Aware!

"THEY SAY"

"They Say" I'm Special, In Need of Care -
"They Say" My Brain is Different & Strange -
"They Say" My Mind isn't Normal Like Yours -
"They Say" I'll Always Stay Young of Mind -
"They Say" I'm Special ... It's True!

HAYLIE-AUTISM
Everywhere I Look
I see All the Things I want to be!
I see Places all over the World where
I can be Anything I Wish to be …
I have Lots of Connections & I can Travel
through Time & never leave My Room …
You See, Everywhere I Look, I can go for Free!
I can Go Alone or take You with Me!

HEY YOU
Dancing & Spinning, Singing & Laughing
are Things I can do & Share with You.
Stay with Me Please … We Can Read a Book!
"Hey You!"
Where Are You Going?
Guess I'll See You in a Little While …
Turn Around if You want to & Look,
I'll Wave & Give You a Great Big Smile!
"Hey You!"

You Know, I'm Pretty Smart for a Girl My Age!
I can Read & Sing & Draw You Know,
I'm a Little Different but Don't Be Afraid …
You Know, I'm Pretty Smart for a Girl My Age
… Did You Know … I Don't Bite!

HAYLIE-AUTISM

My Ins & Outs are All Mixed Up!
What's In is Out, What's Out is In.
I Start, I Stop or Stop & Start ...
Up is Down or Down is Up,
What's Right, What's Wrong
... I Don't Know!
My Ins & Outs are All Mixed Up!

MESS OF CONFUSION

My Outside is a Rainbow of Colors,
My Skin "Caramel" with Brown Hair ...
One Braid only, Washed & Untangled!
Dressed Up & in Style Head to Toe!
I wear My Vans all Rainbows & Colors!
... My Inside is a Mess of Confusion &
Nothing about Everything makes sense!
Noises Echo in My Brain & Never Stop.
Loud Children & Babies Make Me Cry,
I wear My "Kids Ears" to Stop the Sound!
My Inside is a Mess of Confusion &
I Don't Know Why!

HAYLIE-AUTISM
Today I Yell & Scream
... I Don't Know Why.
I Hit My Chin, I Can't Focus,
I Gather My thoughts,
"I'm Sick, I'm Sick, I'm Sick!"
Let's Go on a Mission,
"Are You Scared?"

PLAY IT AGAIN
Over & Over & Over & Over Again!
I Like This One, the Music Talks to Me!
Again & Again & Again & Again ...
Makes Sense to Me ... I Don't Know Why
... So Play it Again ... Sounds Good to Me!

MY WINDOW
I See a Light, Shining So Bright ...
My Window Reflects the Outside to Me
... A World Big & Scary ... A Fright!
My Window is a Life Out of My Reach
... My Window ... Shut Tight!

MIDLIFE MAZE

by Norman Smith

The Events that Form Your Life are a Maze of Personal Decisions affecting How You Exit said "Maze" … At 25 Years You have charted Your path into the Future through Education, Relationships & Career Choices … Your lifestyle is Greatly defined by Country or City Lifestyles, Marriage, Moral Upbringing or Whether You are Manipulated or Driven by Self-Worth … Have You a Conservative, Liberal or Independent Spirit … Have You Traveled or remained Static for Life, Running in Place … Most of All, will You have Great Memories, a Positive Attitude & No Regrets as You Exit the "Midlife Maze" into Your Future Retirement Years!

Printed in the United States
by Baker & Taylor Publisher Services